WRITE RIGHT

Writing
OPINION PAPERS

By Benjamin Proudfit

Gareth Stevens
PUBLISHING

Please visit our website, www.garethstevens.com. For a free color catalog of all our high-quality books, call toll free 1-800-542-2595 or fax 1-877-542-2596.

Library of Congress Cataloging-in-Publication Data

Proudfit, Benjamin.
Writing opinion papers / by Benjamin Proudfit.
p. cm. — (Write right!)
Includes index.
ISBN 978-1-4824-1129-4 (pbk.)
ISBN 978-1-4824-1130-0 (6-pack)
ISBN 978-1-4824-1128-7 (library binding)
1. Essay — Authorship — Juvenile literature. 2. English language — Composition and exercises — Juvenile literature. I. Title.
PN4500.P76 2015
808.4—d23

First Edition

Published in 2015 by
Gareth Stevens Publishing
111 East 14th Street, Suite 349
New York, NY 10003

Copyright © 2015 Gareth Stevens Publishing

Designer: Sarah Liddell
Editor: Kristen Rajczak

Photo credits: Cover, p. 1 Dragon Images/Shutterstock.com; p. 5 TongRo Images/TongRo Images/ Thinkstock.com; p. 7 Jacek Chabraszewski/Shutterstock.com; p. 9 Pressmaster/Shutterstock.com; p. 11 (background) sukiyaki/Shutterstock.com; p. 11 (boy) Samuel Borges Photography/ Shutterstock.com; p. 11 (girl) stockyimages/Shutterstock.com; p. 13 michaeljung/Shutterstock.com; p. 15 imging/Shutterstock.com; p. 17 shironosov/iStock/Thinkstock.com; p. 19 (background) hasan eroğlu/iStock/Thinkstock.com; p. 19 (paper) Paul Vasarhelyi/iStock/Thinkstock.com; p. 21 (background) mexrix/Shutterstock.com; p. 21 (girl) Ronnachai Palas/Shutterstock.com.

Printed in the United States of America

CPSIA compliance information: Batch #CS15GS: For further information contact Gareth Stevens, New York, New York at 1-800-542-2595.

CONTENTS

Words in the glossary appear in **bold** type the first time they are used in the text.

ANY THOUGHTS?

What do you think? That's the main question you need to answer when writing an opinion paper!

An opinion paper is a kind of essay. Opinion papers can be about many topics, such as whether students should have a longer lunch period or who was the greatest US president. In an opinion paper, the writer states their opinion—or what they think—and argues why they think it. Opinion papers are sometimes called "position" papers because you may be taking a position on a topic.

ON THE WRITE TRACK

Your main goal in an opinion paper is to **persuade** the reader of your opinion. Sometimes opinion papers may be called "persuasive" essays, too.

Some opinion papers will ask you to take one side in an issue. Your friend might argue the other side!

DEBATE TODAY

THE ASSIGNMENT

Often, your teachers will tell you what to write about in your opinion paper. The first step of writing it is deciding what you think!

Imagine your school is considering a new dress code. Your teacher may present an **assignment** asking for your opinion on it in a few ways:

- Do you agree with the new dress code?

- Agree or disagree with the new dress code.

- Agree or disagree with this statement: The new dress code is too **strict**.

ON THE WRITE TRACK

When your teacher gives you your assignment, be sure you understand all parts of it. Read the directions carefully, and ask questions if you have them.

CHOOSING A SIDE

Are you unsure of your opinion on the topic you've been assigned? If so, you might need to do some **research**. It will be helpful later when you have to write the paper, too.

See if anyone else has written about your topic. Try to find **credible** sources. Books from the library and websites about the topic are a good place to start. Talking to your parents, friends, and knowledgeable people can help you decide what position to argue in your paper, too.

ON THE WRITE TRACK

When using an Internet source, make sure it's one with a web address ending in .org or .gov, or it's been created by an official group.

If your assignment is about the school dress code and you're unsure what you think about it, try to talk to someone who goes to a school with a similar dress code.

9

STARTING OFF

An opinion paper has three parts: an introduction, a body, and a conclusion.

A strong introduction uses a surprising fact or short story to draw the reader in. This is called the "hook." After the hook, quickly summarize your topic. Depending on the topic, the summary will be one sentence or many.

No other schools in our town have a rule against wearing shorts to school. Under the new dress code, ours will. Last week, the school board proposed this rule as part of a new dress code.

ON THE WRITE TRACK

As you write longer essays, the introduction, body, and conclusion will be separate **paragraphs**.

SPELL IT OUT

The last part of your introduction is the statement of your opinion. This is the topic sentence for your whole essay, telling what you will write about. It should use clear, strong language. Everything else in your essay should support, or hold up, your topic sentence.

Your topic sentence can directly address the assignment your teacher has given.

Assignment: Agree or disagree with the new dress code.

Topic sentence in favor: I agree with the new dress code.

Topic sentence against: I don't agree with the new dress code.

ON THE WRITE TRACK

The topic sentence or statement of opinion is sometimes called the thesis statement. The word "thesis" means a position a person tries to prove through argument.

Another way to agree with the new dress code in a topic sentence could be: The new dress code is a good idea.

IN THE MIDDLE

The body presents facts and observations from your research. They explain why you believe your opinion to be true. Aim to have about three of these supporting ideas.

Outlining the body of your paper will make your argument stronger. Plan the order of your supporting ideas, placing the strongest one last. Then, when you write the essay, use transition words such as "also," "next," and "in addition" to move from one idea to the next.

ON THE WRITE TRACK

The body of an opinion paper can be one paragraph or many. It depends how much support you need to give. Each body paragraph should begin with a topic sentence.

The new dress code is a good idea.
(topic sentence)

easier to get ready
in the morning
(supporting detail)

helps stop bullying
because of clothes
(supporting detail)

keeps focus on schoolwork
(supporting detail)

FINALLY

The last part of an opinion paper is the conclusion. In a single-paragraph essay, it's one or two sentences that sum up your paper. Begin your conclusion with transition words or **phrases** that tell your reader you're coming to an end, such as "overall," "to sum up," or "in conclusion."

In an opinion paper, the conclusion should also answer the question "So what?" Let the reader know why this topic is important or why your opinion matters.

ON THE WRITE TRACK

The conclusion can also include a suggestion or "call to action," which is asking the reader to go do something.

Your conclusion is the last thought you're presenting to the reader. Make it count!

17

DO A DOUBLE CHECK

The last step of writing an essay should always be revision. That means looking over what you've written and changing anything that isn't clear or correct. Use the following questions to revise your opinion paper:

- Do all your sentences begin with a capital letter and end with a period (.), question mark (?), or exclamation point (!)?

- Are all your sentences complete?

- Have you clearly stated your opinion?

- Do each of your details support your topic sentence?

- Have you included transition words to move from one idea to the next?

ON THE WRITE TRACK

A complete sentence has a subject and verb, or action word. The subject is the main person, place, or thing doing the action.

introduction   body

transition   conclusion

No other schools in our town have a rule against wearing shorts to school. Under the new dress code, ours will. Last week, the school board proposed this rule as part of a new dress code. I agree with the new dress code. First, it will make getting ready for school easier since there will be fewer clothes to choose from. Also, students will pay better attention in class. They won't be looking at what other people are wearing as much. In addition, the dress code can help stop bullying over differences in clothing because all students will be wearing clothes that are more alike. Overall, the dress code will be helpful to the students in this school. In the future, the school board should ask the students their opinion before deciding such a big issue, though.

USE YOUR WORK

Your opinion matters, especially if it's supported by facts and observations. Writing an opinion paper for school is great practice for giving your thoughts on a topic in a clear, well-written way.

If you're fired up about a topic, such as the proposal for a stricter dress code, you can use the skills of writing an opinion paper to write about it in the school newspaper. You can argue for or against a new law in a letter to the mayor—or even the president!

ON THE WRITE TRACK

Another way to use your opinion-writing skills is in a blog. "Blog" is short for "web log." Your blog could feature your opinion on movies, books, or the latest news!

CHOOSE YOUR TOPIC

If you can choose any topic for your opinion paper, why not pick something fun? Here are some ideas.

→ What superpower do you think would be the most useful?

→ What's the best kind of pet?

→ Persuade the principal to increase time for lunch or recess.

→ Agree or disagree with the choice of a book to read in class.

→ Explain why you should be class president.

GLOSSARY

assignment: a task or amount of work given to do

controversial: causing arguments

credible: reliable, believable

detail: a small part

outline: to make a plan listing what will be in a piece of writing

paragraph: a group of sentences having to do with one idea or topic

persuade: to make someone believe something by giving good reasons for doing so

phrase: a group of words

research: studying to find something new

strict: having to be obeyed

FOR MORE INFORMATION

BOOKS

Manushkin, Fran. *What Do You Think, Katie? Writing an Opinion Piece with Katie Woo.* North Mankato, MN: Picture Window Books, 2014.

Willis, Meredith Sue. *Blazing Pencils: Writing Stories and Essays.* Millburn, NJ: Montemayor Press, 2013.

WEBSITES

A+ Papers

timeforkids.com/homework-helper/a-plus-papers
Use the Time for Kids Homework Helper for tips on all kinds of writing assignments you might have.

Essays and Other Writing Activities

enchantedlearning.com/essay/topics/if.shtml
Stumped on a topic to write about? This website lists lots of fun essay prompts!

INDEX